Tipton Poetry Journal

Tipton
E

Tipton Poetry Journal, located in Indiana, publishes quality poetry from Indiana and around the world.

Statistics: This issue features 40 poets from the United States (20 different states and the District of Columbia) and 4 poets from Nigeria, Ukraine, United Kingdom and United Arab Emirates.

Our Featured Poem this issue is "The Party's End," written by Jennifer Novotney. Jennifer's poem, which also receives an award of $25, can be found on page 3. The featured poem was chosen by the Board of Directors of Brick Street Poetry, Inc., the Indiana non-profit organization who publishes *Tipton Poetry Journal*.

Barry Harris reviews *Time and Tide: An Atlas for the Grieving* by Denise Thompson-Slaughter

Joyce Brinkman reviews *Open Secrets: The Ultimate Guide to Marketing Your Book*

Cover Photo: *Story Inn, Brown County Indiana* by Brendan Crowley.

Print versions of *Tipton Poetry Journal* are available for purchase through amazon.com.

Barry Harris, Editor

Copyright 2021 by the Tipton Poetry Journal.

All rights remain the exclusive property of the individual contributors and may not be used without their permission.

Tipton Poetry Journal is published by Brick Street Poetry Inc., a tax-exempt non-profit organization under IRS Code 501(c)(3). Brick Street Poetry Inc. publishes the Tipton Poetry Journal, hosts the monthly poetry series *Poetry on Brick Street* and sponsors other poetry-related events.

Tipton Poetry Journal
Contents

Claire Keyes *1*

Fasasi Abdulrosheed Oladipupo *2*

Jennifer Novotney *3*

Timothy Robbins *4*

Leah Browning *5*

Marianne Lyon *6*

Tia Paul-Louis *8*

EG Ted Davis *10*

Sergey Gerasimov *10*

James Green *12*

Gil Arzola *14*

Michael E. Strosahl *15*

CL Bledsoe and Michael Gushue *16*

Patrick T. Reardon *18*

Mary Sexson *20*

Christopher Stolle *21*

Cecil Morris *22*

Mary Hills Kuck *23*

Norbert Krapf *24*

Karla Linn Merrifield *25*

Cindy Buchanan *26*

Caroline Fernandez *27*

Allison Thorpe *28*

Tammy Daniel *29*

Wendy Cleveland *30*

Gayle Compton *32*

Jean Harper *34*

Bruce Levine *34*

Victoria Woolf Bailey *36*

George Looney *36*

Kenneth Pobo *38*

Marie Gray Wise *39*

Michael Estabrook *40*

Bruce Robinson *42*

Gene Twaronite *42*

Christian Ward *44*

Robert Estes *44*

William Heath *46*

James Eric Watkins *48*

Dan Carpenter *49*

Review: Time and Tide: An Atlas for the Grieving by Denise Thompson-Slaughter *52*

Review of Open Secrets:The Ultimate Guide to Marketing Your Book by Tupelo Press *56*

Contributor Biographies *59*

Tipton Poetry Journal

Black Orpheus
Claire Keyes

It's a love story, I tell my older, married sister.
It's won awards. You'll love the music. As we watch
I'm taken by exotic Rio de Janeiro, its grimy favelas
barely containing the anguish of Orpheus.
The characters are black and the music is black and Brazilian,
the rhythms so propulsive the love story blooms
in the melodic body of Orpheus.
Plaintive, he plays his guitar, sings and plans
to retrieve his beloved, a woman so lovely
we know why Hades had to have her
with him in the Underworld.

Around Orpheus wildly costumed people
dance at a street festival invaded by Hades. Sadly,
our hero loses his Euridice again. The music darkens
as he grieves. When it's over, I emerge with my sister
exultant I've discovered a world where passion guides a life
and life without music is inconceivable.
It's a world I want to enter and my sister turns
and says *I didn't think there would be
so many black people.*

Can we talk about this? No. We don't know how.
We don't even try.

Claire Keyes is the author of two collections of poetry: *The Question of Rapture* (Mayapple Press) and *What Diamonds Can Do* (WordTech). Her chapbook, *Rising and Falling*, won the Foothills Poetry Competition. Professor Emerita at Salem State University, she lives in Marblehead, Massachusetts and her poems have been published recently in *Mom Egg Review, Turtle Island, One Art,* and *Persimmon Tree.*

At the Last Zoom Meet

Fasasi Abdulrosheed Oladipupo

At the last zoom meeting, a boy preached to me about death,
He said it is the end, the very end while I know something different

From childhood, my mother said death is a window we must all jump,
A guide taking us on a journey beyond us, a bird, a horse

Driving us to an ancestral home, she said it is not a peace
It is neither a place of grief, it is what we call it, things we write with our hands

And someone chooses to write it as a place of anguish and someone
Chooses a place of bounties, where she would go on Fridays and bargain

More beauty, a lake she would gulp and never be thirsty again,
And another did not choose the anguish nor the bounties

He said, I wanted to be in between, spectating the joy of freedom
Seeing the anguish in sad ending, at the last zoom meet

A boy told me of death as the end to all pains, the end to all worldly griefs,
But my mother said, it can be the desert sun burning us or the morning sun caressing us.

Fasasi Abdulrosheed Oladipupo is a Nigerian poet and a Veterinary Medical Student at University of Ibadan, whose first love is art making. His poems were nominated for the 2021 BOTN and for the 2021 Pushcart Prize. He is an avid reader, who sees poetry in everything, with great interest in storytelling. His works have appeared, or are forthcoming in: *Southern Humanities Review, Oxford Review of Books, Oakland Arts Review, Scrawl Place, Short Vine Journal, Cathexis Northwest Press, South Florida Poetry Journal, Olongo Africa, Roanoke Review, Watershed Review, Panoplyzine, Kissing Dynamite, The Night Heron Barks Review, The Citron Review, Stand Magazine, Louisiana Literature, Obsidian: Literature and Art in the African Diaspora, Welter Journal, Praxis Magazine* and elsewhere.

The Party's End

Jennifer Novotney

Voices, clear at first breath,
echo into the night, fainter & fainter
until ghostly, they disappear
just the end of a laugh, the beginning of a joke
tied loosely together with thin strings.

Even the dog has grown tired of barking
circling our legs one too many times
escaping to clean up scraps around the grill
him now with full belly
letting the mosquitos overtake him.

The kind of bites one gets only from socializing
late into the evening on the moist grass
near the low dip where the creek
winds around the bend, the flash of a lighter
here & there illuminating faces.

But the insects, too, grow tired of eating
falling silent as the first glow
breaks through the horizon
painting the world in pools of brightness
well after the party has ended.

Jennifer Novotney's work appears in *Buddhist Poetry Review, The Beatnik Cowboy,* and *The Vignette Review,* where she was nominated for a Pushcart Prize. She won the 2014 Moonbeam Children's Book Award for her novel, *Winter in the Soul.* She lives in Pennsylvania where she teaches English at a small independent school.

Grass-Scape
Timothy Robbins

These blocks are too safe for dark walks.
Neighborhood watch would call the cops.

Not on me. Wait for fresh light and first
dogs. Then go and commiserate with

lawns variegated by drought. What pre-
Raphaelite wouldn t give his palette for

these lambent blends of burnt umber, raw
and burnt sienna, rare breaths of faded

green? Only a few squares of verdure in
front of the larger houses (grasses with

sugar daddies) and the lot where clover
and thistle breed remind me these colors

are wrong. Eventually a plentiful rain,
though not the rain I need, will come.

Timothy Robbins has been teaching English as a Second Language for 30 years. His poems have appeared in many literary journals and has published five volumes of poetry: *Three New Poets* (Hanging Loose Press), *Denny's Arbor Vitae* (Adelaide Books), *Carrying Bodies* (Main Street Rag Press) *Mother Wheel* (Cholla Needles Press) and *This Night I Sup in Your House* (Cyberwit.net). He lives in Wisconsin with his husband of 24 years.

Velocity

Leah Browning

And then, suddenly, time is moving too fast.
At the hospital, the magazine has Ben Affleck
vacationing with his girlfriend in Puerto Rico,
but on the internet their breakup is old news:
he's already gone through a Jack in the Box
drive-thru with a Playboy Playmate
and Jennifer Garner checked him back
into rehab. In the chair next to me
a woman is using one finger to scroll through
her Twitter feed like a zombie
while a man across the room stabs impatiently
at the buttons of the coffee machine.
Now Demi Lovato has left Cedars-Sinai
and gone to treatment. It seems that
the missing bodies are finally turning up
and the fall shows are almost ready to debut;
wildfires continue to burn up and down the west coast,
and a twin-engine Cessna carrying five people
crashed into the parking lot of a strip mall
and everyone on board was killed.
We're on the cusp of a drought, a flood,
the quake to end all quakes: the earth is loosening,
careening off its axis, waves convulsing
against the shore. Faster, louder.
All around us, they're sounding the alarms,
and still we go on sitting here. Waiting, waiting.

Leah Browning lives in California and is the author of three short nonfiction books and six chapbooks of poetry and fiction. Her work has recently appeared in *Four Way Review, The Broadkill Review, Oyster River Pages, The Forge Literary Magazine, The Threepenny Review, Valparaiso Fiction Review, Watershed Review, Random Sample Review, Belletrist Magazine, Poetry South, The Stillwater Review, Superstition Review, Santa Ana River Review, Newfound, The Homestead Review, Bellows American Review, Coldnoon, Clementine Unbound, The Literary Review,* and elsewhere.
www.leahbrowninglit.com

Queries

Marianne Lyon

      What of life after this one
      query seems incomplete
like dandelion asking if reincarnation is real
as she climbs through charred crack
following devastating inferno

      what is our purpose here
      question appears overwhelming
what if our destiny is connected
what of buds providing nectar
to nourish entire bee colonies
grateful flowers are gifted
with miracle of pollination

      what if all creation is meant to teach
      hold each other
like the desert snake preparing us to shed
like a wave swimming to shore
dissolving effortless into welcoming sand
like leaves crumbling into compost
allowing indebted garden to thrive

      what if our purpose is to rebirth love
      alive every awakened moment
question is staggering   unfathomable
in my monotonous daily grind
but what of lone worm when she dies
is she alive in satisfied bird
does the rain know nirvana
when he swells thirsty roots

      what if I dissolve into all I love
too deep a question   love is hard to describe
what if I sing Beatle song   *love is all we need*
and it becomes a bridge for those too tired to walk
what if incanting   *we shall overcome*
grows a glint of compassion for those yet to be born

Pines at Night

Marianne Lyon

Aging wanderer   taken to explore night
at mossy fringe of pine forest
between snaking valley and foothills
faithful guardians   Rockies Mountains

In quiet sanctuary stoic trees gather
tang of incense given to sap
insects hum vespers
the tall one   a preacher
others shoulder together
like books on high shelf
slight wind licks them
branches reverently bow
like string orchestra after applause

I walk on   meet another tangle
limbs play rippling wind
ballerinas dance ringlets
some grow big bellies
others   bearded old men

A lone tree amens me
my knees sink in soft needles
his branches   bubbling prayer flags
rejoice like pilgrim hands
taken to lift   rise

I pray aimless breeze to dance me
anoint my heavy limbs
sway me like a Holy Roller
I look up at his tallest reach
listen for the ineffable
of what he knows   but my
searching eyes see only an
infinite sweep of spangled stars

Marianne Lyon has been a music teacher for 43 years. After teaching in Hong Kong she returned to the Napa Valley and has been published in various literary magazines and reviews. Nominated for the Pushcart Award 2016. She has spent time teaching in Nicaragua. She is a member of the California Writers Club, Solstice Writers in St. Helena California and an Adjunct Professor at Touro University Vallejo California. She was awarded the Napa Country Poet Laureate 2021 title.

If Only

Tia Paul-Louis

If only times weren't passing

you'd love me. You'd love
yawning bells, chimes,
      clocks with eyes but no hands
and ghost alarms.
If only times were blessings

I'd be your kind. You'd love.
You'd want me as is:
      blue-veiled maiden, quiet with
      a flame-like portrait.
Your arms would frame me.

But the hours fall like an avalanche.
I'm in your way,
and in your final breath, you'd push me
off the cliff.

Little White
Tia Paul-Louis

There's a little white rose in my garden
that won't get pulled and refuses to be fed.
It hangs with a sass that pricks
my thumb and index like a porcupine.
It whips its head to the side
when I frown. And if I stare too long,
it tucks under the bushes as if
their arms were guardians, and I was
a thief. But when I whistle
Beethoven, it comes out, apologetic,
wanting to dance
in the palm of my hands.

Born in the Caribbean and raised in the U.S., **Tia Paul-Louis** began writing songs at age 11 then experimented with poetry during high school. She earned a BA in English/Creative Writing from the University of South Florida along with a M.F.A in Creative Writing from National University in California. Her works have appeared in literary magazines such as *The Voices Project, Ethos Literary Journal,* and *Rabbit Catastrophe Review.* Some of her favorite authors and poets include Langston Hughes, Emily Dickinson, Maya Angelou and Edgar Allan Poe. Apart from writing, Paul-Louis enjoys music, photography, acting and cooking, though she mostly finds herself and others through poetry.

How shall he respond
EG Ted Davis

It is at its melting point
(the chocolate that is),
as it dribbled from
the sides of his mouth,
no control without
his dentures in.
But the pleasure was
seen within in his pupils…

How shall he respond
upon seeing angels.

EG Ted Davis is a semi-retiree who resides in Boise, Idaho and has written poetry since back in the 80's with work appearing in various online literary journals and websites in the US and the UK.

An Ambulance That Is Late
Sergey Gerasimov

It's not dawn yet.
An ambulance that is late
has stopped in front of the gray bulk
of the hospital building,
at some wilted bushes,
under an acacia tree, pruned
into the form of a naked brain.

The door is opened wide like a gigantic mouth
lit from the inside,
toothless, distorted with pain
screaming as silently as the Munch's painting .
The ambulance that is late
looks like a drunken girl scout
throwing up
onto some dusty steps of
an unfamiliar porch,
embarrassed,
not remembering at all after what
for what
and with whom.
But the sky is so vast,
so clear,
and the air is so still
that you can see
souls
that flutter,
flying up,
falling upwards
over the hospital roof.
They sparkle, tumble,
collide with each other
like a handful of small coins
thrown in water.

Sergey Gerasimov is a Ukraine-based writer. His stories and poems have appeared in *Adbusters, Clarkesworld Magazine, Strange Horizons, J Journal, Triggerfish Critical Review*, among others. His last book is *Oasis* published by Gypsy Shadow.

The Perseids: A Triptych
James Green

I wake at midnight and drive to an open field,
away from lights, where a low-slung moon
in first quarter sits on the top of a pole barn
and I wait until the first one drops into view,

flashes through a field of stars, then vanishes.
I think of Hawkins and star-swallowing portals
leading to the other side of the nightscape
he said we can know only as post Newtonian,

which I do not understand, so my mind
strays to Whitman, who grew weary while
listening to the learned astronomer's lecture
overflowing with theories and calculations

then wandered off into the moist night-air
and looked up at the stars in silence.

~

One streaks from the breast of Perseus,
and another, flaming fragments of comet-dust
raining from a leaden sky – the Perseids.
Ah, Perseus, Andromeda's hero,

all around fixer of others' messes,
as well as some of his own. His stars have names
as old as the Tower of Babel. *Algol. Mirfak.
Atik.* They glow in the path of Cassiopeia

who wheels across the sky. They bask
in the shine of Andromeda awaiting rescue.
Cetus lurks on the south horizon where a volley
of flaming missiles lands on his back.

A story we all know. If not the plot, the themes:
Pride, Reprisal. Sacrifice. Deliverance.

~

I sip the last of some wine from a paper cup
and wonder what sound, what celestial music,
these star-sparks make as they startle and skip
across the firmament, what harmony echoes

through the Milky Way, a holy fire
we try to measure in (of all things)
light years. These stars that witnessed creation,
what do they know that we do not?

Somewhere in the distance a dog barks
at the shadows of a house where a couple
lies asleep in one another's arms.
A birdsong drifts singularly across the night.

One more falls into a stand of trees.
Cassiopeia tilts back on her throne.

James Green has worked as a naval officer, deputy sheriff, high school English teacher, professor of education, and administrator in both public schools and universities. Recipient of two Fulbright grants, he has served as a visiting scholar at the University of Limerick in Ireland and the National Chung Cheng University in Taiwan. In addition to academic publications, including three books, Green is the author of three chapbooks of poetry and a fourth, *Long Journey Home*, is forthcoming after winning the Charles Dickson Chapbook Contest sponsored by the Georgia Poetry Society., Individual poems have appeared in literary magazines in England, Ireland, and the United States. He resides in Muncie, Indiana.

The Fiftieth Reunion Of The Class Of 71
Gil Arzola

I'd like to sit down with my best friend
in the eighth grade who drank himself
to death and have a cup of coffee.
I'd like to talk about the weather and
        drive past the corn fields he used to work.
        Maybe we'd walk into them not talking about
        anything important,
        just breathing in the green and
        listening to birds argue in trees.

That would be important enough.

I'd like to meet (by chance), the pretty blonde girl
who died of cancer and sat two desks away from me
in english class. I'd say I was sorry that she's dead.
I'd tell her about the crush I had on her
since the second grade. But that I was too shy to mention.

        I'd say I was sorry that I hadn't.

I'd like to take a walk in the woods where the boy in high school that
I barely knew shot himself with a shotgun jumping
out of tree. That was the story. But we didn't buy it.
I'd say I was sorry for all of that and for
pushing him so hard in the hall one day that
he fell, arms and legs flailing and falling in all directions like autumn leaves.
I'd like to tell him that I didn't intend to push so hard.

Gil Arzola is the second son of a migrant worker living in Valparaiso, Indiana with his wife Linda. He was named Poet Of The Year by Passager Press in 2019. His first book of poetry *Prayers of Little Consequence* was published in 2020. Rattle published a chapbook *The Death of Migrant Worker* in September of 2021 after selecting it from 2000 submissions for their annual prize. A story *Losers Walk,* originally published by Chaluer, was nominated for a Pushcart Award in 2018. His work has appeared in *Whetstone, Palabra, Crosswinds, Tipton Poetry Journal, Passager, Slab* and *The Elysian Review* among others.

Spilt

Michael E. Strosahl

"I don't usually wear red,"
she said as she
tried to clean up the stain—
bleaching out the
blood on blood—
"It tends to wash me out."

Her face was already pale,
edges failing to a
memory fog—
I struggle to remember
when she last showed a blush
beyond what she spilled—
she was soaked into everything.

She burned off
like a mist into morning,
eyes streamed with ashes
as she made her escape
with the late autumn winds.

"I should have married in white,"
she whispered,
her lips touched in wine.

The stain stubborn and fast set,
her voice fading into the woods—
the blood went everywhere.

Michael E. Strosahl is a midwestern river-born poet, originally from Moline, Illinois, now living in Jefferson City, Missouri. Besides several appearances in the *Tipton Poetry Journal*, Maik's work has appeared in *Flying Island, Bards Against Hunger* projects, on buses, in museums and online at *indianavoicejournal, poetrysuperhighway* and *projectagentorange*. Maik also has a weekly poetry column at the online blog *Moristotle & Company*.

How to Hypnotize a Chicken
CL Bledsoe and Michael Gushue

Begin by grasping its plutonium rods
and holding them firmly extended behind
its breasts. Maintain eye contact while humming
Delibes' flower duet. This will ensure the chicken
is distracted trying to remember where it knows
that from. Was it a problematic Netflix show?
Was it a stylish waiting room? Be sure not
to chafe its feathers with your Hazmat suit,
otherwise, you'll angry up the meat.
A chicken is like any other kind of machine,
it wants to belong, and to be reassured
that its place in the world is secure.
Start near the chicken's beak and suggest
that anxiety is a social construct.
Are chickens afraid of losing control?
Most would rather have a reassuring
authority figure lull them into a relaxing
fugue state. Ask your chicken
to fill out a brief questionnaire.
Peck once for disagree, twice for strongly agree.
Your chicken will enter a soporific state.
Practice voter disenfranchisement
and see if it reacts. If it does, you'll need
to continue the process. Have it visualize
ducks massaging its sore legs, pigs bathing
it in lavender and sandalwood essence.
Your chicken will start to recall its past lives.
It's a magician. The curtain opens, revealing
a hushed audience. Its assistant asks
for a volunteer from the audience.
A duck leaves its seat, mounts the stairs
onto the stage, but the chicken's mind
is a blank, it knows only that a vital truth
has been stolen from chickens everywhere.

December

CL Bledsoe and Michael Gushue

Your feet will always be cold
because of poor circulation, holes
in all your socks, severed toes.
Everything you'll ever want to know
will be at your fingertips which means
you'll never know anything
because you'll be too easily distracted.
Dogs won't trust you, and those that do
will be the dumb ones you don't want to pet.
Children will yell things across parking lots
about your weight and race, and you'll begin
to understand that you will never become
or even create anything truly beautiful.
How could you? The pretty ones were right
all along, just being. Intelligence is of no value
in this world, but salesmen know the secret
of lightning. No one will ever love you
the way your mother did, but she died
so young, and you'll live so long.

Raised on a rice and catfish farm in eastern Arkansas, **CL Bledso**e is the author of more than twenty books, including the poetry collections *Riceland, Trashcans in Love, Grief Bacon,* and his newest, *Driving Around, Looking in Other People's Windows*, as well as his latest novels *Goodbye, Mr. Lonely* and the forthcoming *The Saviors*. Bledsoe co-writes the humor blog *How to Even*, with Michael Gushue located here: https://medium.com/@howtoeven. His own blog, *Not Another TV Dad*, is located here: https://medium.com/@clbledsoe. He's been published in hundreds of journals, newspapers, and websites that you've probably never heard of. Bledsoe lives in northern Virginia with his daughter.

Michael Gushue is co-founder of the nanopress *Poetry Mutual*. His books are *Pachinko Mouth* (Plan B Press), *Conrad* (Silver Spoon Press), *Gathering Down Women* (Pudding House Press), and—in collaboration with CL Bledsoe—*I Never Promised You A Sea Monkey* (Pretzelcoatl Press). He lives in the Brookland neighborhood of Washington, D.C.

Crossroad

Patrick T. Reardon

Obadiah went out at dawn to the crossroad of Kindness Avenue and Truth Highway.

As the sun rose, he stood with his thumb out as the priest's car drove past. "Carrying the Host!" A better passenger, surely, lighter, at least.

In the day's first rays, Obadiah flagged at his father's car. "Got all the kids in here, too crowded!" He was frowning.

Obadiah waved his arms at his mother's car, driven by his scarred brother with her holding the gun to his head. "You hurt us!" To which brother, impossible to say.

He was walking, head down, away when the tall seven-year-old boy on his bike ran into him from behind, stood over him on the sidewalk to see the blood at his eye and ran — hid in the back bedroom until the cops came.

Five Songs

Patrick T. Reardon

He restyled the opening
words of *Genesis* as a
country-western song,
let there be light and
all that, fruitful and
multiply — drinking,
trucks and death
would come later.

For a heavy metal
band, he composed a
horror song about a
baby trapped by city
demons: "Don't bring
me down!" Bowie-ish.

At a store on Mount
Horeb Street, under the
el, he found the sheet
music for somebody's
unfinished *Requiem*
and wrote an ending.

His folk album contained
a suicide ballad titled
"The Lost Boy and His
Brother," panned as
dark bleak grim.

"The Lost Tribes" went
on forever, likened to a
Yoko Ono screech, and
to Lennon's primal
"Mother," a dispatch
from bowels of darkness.

Patrick T. Reardon, a three-time Pushcart Prize nominee living in Chicago, is the author of nine books, including the poetry collection *Requiem for David* and *Faith Stripped to Its Essence*. His poetry has appeared in *America, Rhino, Main Street Rag, The Write Launch, Meat for Tea, Under a Warm Green Linden* and many others. He has two poetry collections in 2021: *Puddin: The Autobiography of a Baby, a Memoir in Prose-poems* (Third World Press) and *Darkness on the Face of the Deep* (Kelsay Books).

The Words
Mary Sexson

What do you tell a daughter
on the eve of her 37th birthday?

That you love her?
                Unquestionably
That you are grateful?
                Yes.
That you are
inextricably entwined with her?
                Of course.

So what new words
can be spoken on this day?

Most importantly, tell her
            you are glad that she lived,
            from a cord twisted
            around her neck
            as you tried to push her
            out into this world,
            to her days at a rehab center
            shaking off the hold
            of her addiction, and all
            the near misses between them.

Tell her you embrace it,
        that you take it into your heart.
Tell her
        that you learn the truth about love
        every time you are with her.

Mary Sexson is the author of *103 in the Light, Selected Poems 1996-200* (Restoration Press, 2004) and coauthor of *Company of Women, New and Selected Poems*, (Chatter House Press, 2013). A 3 time Pushcart Prize nominee, her poetry appears or is forthcoming in *Flying Island, New Verse News, The World We Live(d) In, Hoosier Lit, Last Stanza Poetry Journal, High Veld Poetry Review, and Anti-Heroin Chic*. Her poetry is part of the INverse Poetry Archive, a collection of poetry by Indiana poets, housed at the Indiana State Library.

Silhouette & Spotlight
Christopher Stolle

a glossary

Alabaster: a light caught in amber
Beam: an unregulated shard of light

Crepuscule: the moment when lovers kiss
Darkness: funereal shroud worn by the moon

Electrode: whispered gossip about neon signs
Flicker: laughter emanating from fireflies

Gloom: when dusk morphs into dawn
Haze: a portmanteau of hope and blaze

Illuminate: to cast a squinted glance at sunrise
Joule: how long your limelight will last

Kilowatt: a superficial measurement of aura light
Luminary: someone who carries an Olympic torch

Monochromatic: stars committed to one performance
Nocturnal: those who dream before sunset

Opaque: the color of a hardened broken heart
Penumbra: a crescent moon with low battery power

Quasar: an infinite infant universe of stars
Radiance: how stunned people are at your brilliance

Shadow: the quintessential representation of your soul
Tenebrous: the moment when the soliloquy ends

Umbra: covering yourself with obscurity
Voltage: the symbiotic merging of human bodies

Wavelength: how far you go to greet someone
X-ray: reversing your electrons to find ailments

Yttrium: an element that turns light and dark into gray
Zenith: the point when the sun shines brightest

Christopher Stolle's writing has appeared most recently in *Tipton Poetry Journal, Flying Island, Last Stanza Poetry Journal, The New Southern Fugitives, The Alembic, Gravel, The Light Ekphrastic, Sheepshead Review,* and *Plath Poetry Project.* He's an editor for DK Publishing and he lives in Richmond, Indiana.

All My Lives
Cecil Morris

This morning I imagine parallel universes
running side by side through space and time or maybe twisting
around each other like separate fibers braided in rope
or overlapping like twine wound tight in gigantic balls
or like fresh laundry stacked in folds of possibility
or maybe like multitudinous and invisible
yet discrete str2ams of data streaking through fiber optic
cables. I imagine how my infinitely varied
lives might be screaming along simultaneously,
each parallel me unaware of the numberless
other mes as similar as all the shades of gray,
as different as black and white, each blind, each oblivious
to the way every single choice cascades consequences,
every action or inaction a singularity,
its own big bang of multifarious forkings,
until, limitless as photons, I travel uncounted
roads, all my lives in action at one time, each a secret
unknowable by the others. So, spiraling somewhere
across the universes, Rhonda met the eighth grade me
at the Square for ice cream and liked me enough to meet again
and again until we wed and somewhere else I died young
when my mother did not yank me from river's rush and throw
me on the bank where I flopped and gasped like a stunned fish
and somewhere else entirely I am still living the life
where my first wife, my true heart, did not lose her life to cancer,
where we grow old together and watch our children raise their children.

Cecil Morris lives in California and is retired after 37 years of teaching high school English. He now tries writing himself what he spent so many years teaching others to understand and enjoy. He likes ice Cream too much and cruciferous vegetables too little. He has had a handful of poems published in *2River View, Cobalt Review, English Journal, The Ekphrastic Review, The Midwest Quarterly, Poem*, and other literary magazines.

November

Mary Hills Kuck

Eventually this dismal rain will stop,
that cancelled out the halcyon days
of just last week when we forgot
the month while playing
in the papery leaves
that sifted down
like snow.
Who could blame me if I wanted
back the balmy air, the breeze,
the copper trees, the cheerful sky,
the thought that winter is delayed?
But that can't be, don't think of it.
Winter always follows fall,
just as you and I both age.

Having retired from teaching English and Communications, first in the US and for many years in Jamaica, **Mary Hills Kuck** now lives with her family in Massachusetts. She has received a Pushcart Prize Nomination and her poems have appeared in *Connecticut River Review, Hamden Chronicle, SIMUL: Lutheran Voices in Poetry, Caduceus, The Jamaica Observer Bookends, Fire Stick: A Collection of New & Established Caribbean Poets, the Aurorean, Tipton Poetry Journal, Burningwood Literary Journal, Slant* and *Main Street Rag*, and others.

She Hummed

Norbert Krapf

When I woke in my bedroom
above the kitchen where she
was preparing the breakfast
I could hear her hum happily.

When I came downstairs she
was still humming about
the beginning of another day.
If your mother hums the day in

you have no right to mope, no
matter what you have dreamed.
So I too hummed, quietly, as she
said good morning like a happy bird.

So I guess I chirped back, glad to
have a mama bird so happy to be
alive in her own kitchen that I
did my own kind of singing too.

A former Indiana Poet Laureate, **Norbert Krapf** has published fourteen poetry collections, the most recent *Indiana Hill Country Poems* and *Southwest by Midwest*. *My Homecomings: A Writer's Memoir*, covering the fifty years of his writing and publishing life, will appear next year. Krapf has also produced a poetry and jazz CD with pianist-composer Monika Herzig, *Imagine* and also performs poetry and blues with Gordon Bonham. See also www.krapfpoetry.net.

How Thin the Tissue between Past and Present
Karla Linn Merrifield

butterfly-wing fragile
one blink
I am in my study writing
amid the clutter of lives on paper
in the company of a brown bat
partaking warmth
small rent in the fabric of his webbing
his small mammal heart throbbing
from the effort of crawling
wicker basket to space heater shelter
closer to me
red-blooded companion

another blink
I am in another book-lined room
fifty years ago
shelves towering over me
teen tryst in the stacks
necking petting rubbing
his groin on my pelvis
spines of oversized volumes
pressing into my spine
no librarian no patron no voyeur
but the dust-cover odalisque
by Picasso who *looked like me*

Karla Linn Merrifield Karla Linn Merrifield has had 900+ poems appear in dozens of journals and anthologies. She has 14 books to her credit. Following her 2018 *Psyche's Scroll* (Poetry Box Select) is the 2019 full-length book *Athabaskan Fractal: Poems of the Far North* from Cirque Press. She is currently at work on a poetry collection, *My Body the Guitar*, inspired by famous guitarists and their guitars; the book is slated to be published in December 2021 by Before Your Quiet Eyes Publications Holograph Series (Rochester, NY).

What I Want
Cindy Buchanan

It's fall, but warm. My mother and I
remove coats while we collect leaves
which she later displays, their veins
and crisp edges arrayed on her glass table.

And then: *What do you want,* she asks.
Her hand sweeps towards knickknacks,
books, furniture. The spoon in my teacup
rattles. *Your mahogany chest*

is what I answer, but what I mean is
I want me, age three,
leaning against that ornate chest, her
majorette's baton clutched in one hand

my feet splendid in tasseled white cowboy boots.
I don't remember this. It's a memory
forged from a photo my mother keeps—
a black and white taken before the seasons

when batons bruised, boots kicked with hate—
before I learned wooden boxes hold more
than ecru doilies, crocheted blankets,
certificates of birth.

Cindy Buchanan grew up in Alaska and has lived in Seattle since graduating from Gonzaga. Work has been published in *Evening Street Review, The MacGuffin, Rabid Oak, Hole in the Head Review,* and *Chestnut Review,* and is upcoming in *Main Street Rag.* An avid runner and hiker with a deep interest in Buddhist philosophy and Zen meditation practice, she has completed the Camino de Santiago in Spain, the Coast to Coast Walk in England, and the Milford Walking Track in New Zealand.

Unleashed
Caroline Fernandez

Nothing like
walking past
the chain-link trail from you
the waist-deep pit in you
the sky-high climb to you
the spools of morse code
winding 'round you.
Where once I followed
your many faces
with an untethered compass,
now I stay on track as
you leak out of me.

Slow, thick oil spills from
the pores of my slackened flesh
the teeth marks along my wrists
from my gnarled ankles
the gums of my brittle grin
the scabs threading my knees.
Coarse, scorching tar
hardens on me as
snowflakes of dead skin hover,
and walls of locusts surround
the lion's den as it begins to stir.
I must limp quietly.

Caroline Fernandez is an Indo-Canadian journalist and performer based in Dubai. Her reporting has ranged from media analysis to arts, business, and culture, and she has also contributed to and led several social justice projects around sexuality and inequality. She has been published in various news publications including *TimeOut Dubai*, toronto.com and *Communicate*. She's performed on stages across Toronto, Montreal, Bangalore and Dubai. She is also the founder of the multimedia news platform *Kerosene Digital*. Currently she is an MFA candidate at Vermont College and is working on a collection of essays and poetry.

Imagining Ellis Island While Getting My First Covid Shot

Allison Thorpe

Our ship has landed
Our number called
We clutch our identity cards
Like thin fluttering hearts
Body after body after body we totter
Forward like lumbering turtles
Our masks shells of isolation
Conversation a forgotten cleverness

    Keep 6' apart   *Go there*   *Stand here*

Our line stutters dull hallways
Funnels toward the next unseen bend
And the next until we are just trundled
Atoms seeking a skeletal reality
Shuffling our baggage like hope
Then final deliverance into a cavernous room

    Name?   *Sign here*   *Which arm?*

A woman presses a sticker onto each lapel
Ushers us back into the world
We had forgotten or maybe never knew
The sky blue rich and sun soused
A land smelling of lilacs and possibilities
Where fair winds sail through trees like freedom

Allison Thorpe lives in Lexington, Kentucky. Her collection, *Reckless Pilgrims*, was published in 2021 by Broadstone Books.

First Treatment

Tammy Daniel

The cancer concierge calls
my name, escorts me to the first
of four treatment rooms
she quaintly refers to as a *cubby*.

I crawl into that word *cubby*
envisioning a board of mind-control educators
convinced its usage would provide patients
with a sense of comfort, cuddly as naptime
on the first day of kindergarten.

Then, as if I were a child toting
a small stack of coloring books, I'm told
to select a seat. In an act of defiance,
I forego the offer of a snack or warm blanket.

Instead, I deposit myself on the sandy beach
of a vinyl recliner basking under the warm
rays of a sun-soaked window

where I'll work on my tan
until the afternoon bell rings.

Tammy Daniel was selected as one of New Voices of 2015 by The Writers Place in Kansas City, Missouri. She was a finalist in the Davis Grove Haiku and Nature Poetry Contest, and her work has appeared in *I-70 Review, Touch: The Journal of Healing, The Ekphrastic Review, Anthology on Aging: The Shining Years, Dying Dahlia Review, Wild Goose Poetry Review, Red River Review, Rusty Truck, Ink Sweat and Tears*, and the Johnson County Library.

Potter's Field, April 6, 2020
Wendy Cleveland

From juvie to jail awaiting trial, he's now a COVID grave digger
who rides the daily ferry from Rikers to Hart Island with benches
of masked men crowded together, quiet as the boat churns black
water, wavelets fanning behind in a perfect V. Pandemic ravages
the city, killing rich and poor, men and women, young and old,
numbers growing, no funerals to bury the dead. Plain pine boxes
are built to claim the unclaimed tucked inside, no time to wait,
no hands to hold or embalm, no prayers prayed for their journey
to that elusive resting place. His hands that have dipped into tills
lie still until they're given a shovel and the promise of $6 an hour.
The boat docks and he shuffles on to dry land, silent, observing
the gaping trench that swallows 1,165 identical wooden caskets.
He climbs to the top of the newly dug mountain of dirt
where he hears the churning ferry deliver its cargo of cadavers,
the foreman yelling above the backhoe *four-zero-dash-three,*
the chink of dirt and rock raining over three tiers of pine.

Berks Heim
Wendy Cleveland

It's hardly home but she will live out her life
lying in a hospital bed by a window facing east,
morning sun coaxing scarlet cardinals
to a window feeder fat with seed.
Her husband was the only man who touched her
and now a stranger tells her to undress,
slides his cold fingers down her neck,
probes her throat and ears, presses a stethoscope
to her white chest, breasts lapping her belly.
Breathe he whispers, and she exhales a gasp,
grasping the bedrail, her teared eyes wary
like a rabbit caught in the teeth of a trap.
Even those dwelling in dementia feel danger
like a pebble in the throat —
these faces, family, this room a home.

Wendy Cleveland is a retired NYS high school English teacher who now teaches an ekphrastic poetry class for the Auburn University lifelong learning program, and a member of the Alabama Writers' Forum. Her work has appeared in *Persimmon Tree, Red Rock Review,* and *Glass Mountain*, among other journals. In 2016 Solomon & George published her poetry collection, *Blue Ford.*

Call Me Ishmael
Gayle Compton

Once I believed in Endymion.

Once Keats, the bard of joy,
sang to me in "mused rhyme."

I read *Moby Dick* in a front porch swing
and heard the sea's rolling symphony
beneath the swinging bridge.

Once my mother drew water
and the rusty voice of the well chain
was the *Pequoid's*
farewell to Nantucket.

Hanging off a C & O coal gon,
I blew in at the Cape,
bearded, unbathed and swarthy.

With my clothes in a cardboard box
I rode the Greyhound bus
to the mills
of East Chicago, Indiana.

I saw hellfire trundled
on an ingot buggy
and breathed the
sulphurous breath of Satan.

Clinging to the wheel of a '54 Mercury
like Queequeg's floating coffin,
I found at last
the return road to Peabrook.

Abraham, my dear old redbone,
rose stiff-legged from the porch,
whining and stretching,
his eyes full of memory and forgiveness.

Gayle Compton, a hillbilly from Eastern Kentucky, lives up the river from where Randall McCoy is buried and attended college on the hill where "Cotton Top" Mounts was hanged. With deep affection, he tells the story of Appalachia's common people, allowing them to speak, without apology, in their own colorful language. His prize-winning stories, poems, and essays have appeared most recently in *Sow's Ear, Now and Then, New Southerner, Blue Collar Review, Kentucky Review,* and *Main Street Rag* anthologies.

Grace
Jean Harper

there's a stalk of volunteer corn in the bed of azaleas
from last year's harvest – the combine worked through
the rows on a blustery day, the southerly wind relentless –

and little Grace is pregnant, due in a month – she isn't saying
who the father is – last week her Girl Scout troop threw
her a baby shower: diapers and wipes, a teether, booties –

that wind stirred up everything loose from the fields, pushed
great piles of husks into our fencerows, into the sides of the barns
kernels the size of baby teeth littered gardens and pastures and roads –

once, long ago, I lost a child I didn't know I was carrying – it was mostly
an uneventful thing but for the blood and the pain – pain
that cut like a knife, but not exactly like a knife, that kind of pain –

there was even a car seat for Grace's baby and one of those toys
that hangs over a crib to wink and sing and light up the night
with soothing rainbow colors for the baby – the baby – the baby –

Jean Harper's writing has appeared in *The Florida Review, North American Review, Iowa Review*, and elsewhere. She is has received fellowships from the National Endowment for the Arts, the Indiana Arts Commission, and been in residence at Yaddo, MacDowell, and the Virginia Center for the Creative Arts. She lives in northeast Indiana.

The Journey of Waiting
Bruce Levine

The day slowly ebbing away
Another checked off
On the journey of waiting

A week gone by
Sleeping away hours
Daylight waning
'Til another night
And another dawn

Empty moments
Filled with empty moments
Unresolved

Fanciful meanderings
Daydreams of a happy future
Sewn together with gossamer thread
On a tapestry yet created

Counting the chimes
As the clock strikes
The house in the dark
An elusive refrain
Against a background of emptiness

Holding on to the ephemeral
Watching an empty screen
Metadata floating in cyberspace
As the longing continues
In a vacuum of reality

Filling the void
And the empty days
With waiting

Bruce Levine, a 2019 Pushcart Prize Poetry Nominee, has spent his life as a writer of fiction and poetry and as a music and theatre professional. Over 300 of his works are published in over 25 on-line journals including *Ariel Chart, Friday Flash Fiction, Literary Yard;* over 30 print books including *Poetry Quarterly, Haiku Journal, Dual Coast Magazine*, and his shows have been produced in New York and around the country. Six eBooks are available from Amazon.com. His work is dedicated to the loving memory of his late wife, Lydia Franklin. He lives in Maine with his dog, Daisy. Visit him at www.brucelevine.com.

Polishing Old Nails
Victoria Woolf Bailey

The sun damage, the dark splotches,
began in her teens, continued unabated,
she, never one for sun screen or lotion. The bumps,
on the top joint of her index fingers, began in her fifties.
No problem, the doctors said. Not much to be done,
they all said, as the hands turned to gnarled roots,
the skin to fine leather. And now I paint her nails
pink while she tells me about the baby she lost,
the girl she once held.

Victoria Woolf Bailey lives in Kentucky and is recently retired. Her first full-length collection, *Cannibalism and the Copenhagen Interpretation: a Love Story* will be released in March 2022 by Finishing Line Press.

Of Drive-Ins and Cowboy Bars
George Looney

after Walker Evans' Garage in Southern City Outskirts, 1936

The three women dressed to kill can't
go anywhere till this Cherokee
mechanic figures out what's wrong
with the engine. One of them's listening to
what could be some faint and ancient chant
she hears in the cool air of the garage.
Maybe the fevered ghost of a Choctaw

who drank himself out of his loneliness
into a different kind of being
alone. She seems to be staring at
the oil-stained floor of the dark garage
and now, without meaning to, she's humming
a tune the sad ghost has been singing
to her. Though the lyrics are a language

she's never heard, she knows it's a story
of lovers crying out in the back seats
of cars that aren't theirs while on the screen
large enough the light's visible
for miles in this sorry, flat county
cowboys slaughter warriors and women
hug children even in death. Love finds
what desperate niches it can in this

world. One of her friends will hear her shout this
later, after the Cherokee has fixed
the engine and they have found a saloon
with sawdust on the floor and cowboy music
blaring loud enough almost nothing
can be heard over it. She'll nod and toast
to love, cowboys, and a nice set of wheels.

George Looney is the founder of the BFA in Creative Writing Program at Penn State Erie, editor-in-chief of the international literary journal *Lake Effect*, translation editor of *Mid-American Review*, and co-founder of the original Chautauqua Writers' Festival. He has published several books, most recently *The Itinerate Circus: New and Selected Poems 1995-2020* (Red Mountain Press, 2020), *The Worst May Be Over* (Elixer Press, 2020), and *Ode to the Earth in Translation* (Red Mountain Press, 2021).

Bobolinko Doesn't
Kenneth Pobo

talk much about where he grew up.
He changes the subject
like it's dirty underwear.
Somewhere in southern Indiana.

He says his mother is a warped
Window sill. His dad is silent
as a Patoka River marbled
salamander. Bobolinko left

for San Francisco at 22
but couldn't afford it.
Three years of restaurant work.
Three years of eating doughnuts
from trash cans. Three years
of streetcars dissipating
like clouds. Now he's here
in Wausau. We may be compatible
as scrambled eggs and sausage.

Pines guard us. We need guards
since time carries a pistol
and sneaks up behind us.

Kenneth Pobo is the author of 21 chapbooks and 9 full-length collections. Recent books include *Bend of Quiet* (Blue Light Press), *Loplop in a Red City* (Circling Rivers), *Dindi Expecting Snow* (Duck Lake Books), *Wingbuds* (cyberwit.net), and *Uneven Steven* (Assure Press). *Opening* from Rectos Y Versos Editions is forthcoming. Human rights issues, especially as they relate to the LGBTQIA+ community, are also a constant presence in his work. In addition to poetry, he also writes fiction and essays. For the past thirty-plus years he taught at Widener University in Pennsylvania and retired in 2020.

On the Disservice of Dreams

Marie Gray Wise

I stayed in bed an extra ten minutes
because I'd dreamed of kissing Brad Pitt
and wanted to hold that image as long as I could.

This wasn't wacky *Burn After Reading* Brad
or the slick *Ocean's Eleven* one
Just regular neighbor-next-door Brad
except he was sitting in *my* driveway on a stool,
and so intent on an object
that he turned over and over in his lap
that he didn't look up when I kissed him.

The offhandedness of a quick kiss
on my way to the store made it enchanting—
more believable than hanging on his arm
walking down a red carpet.

Besides all the off-facts of the dream—
being too old for Brad and long married with children—
I faced a day that couldn't possibly meet
this dream's optimistic expectations.
Nothing lovely and fuzzy coming my way—
only sparing with my scratchy-voiced boss
writing some lame package copy
and copying some lame faxes—

 and how was I going to bring myself to do that now?

Marie Gray Wise lives in New Jersey. She has been published previously in *Tipton Poetry Journal* and in *I-70 Review, English Journal, U.S. 1 Worksheets, The Café Review, Naugatuck River Review, The Paterson Literary Review* and *Grey Sparrow Journal.*

Give or Take

Michael Estabrook

Don't waste time worrying
about what you can't change
or fix she tells me all the time.

The fancy-pants astrophysicist
with the big glasses and crazy hair explains
in logical scientific detail
that in 5 billion years (give or take)
our Milky Way Galaxy will collide
with our neighbor
the so much larger Andromeda Galaxy
and be torn apart.
Oh no! I think and begin to worry
but abruptly realize – 5 billion years, seriously!
Even I can't be that stupid to worry
about something 5 billion years down the road
I tell myself as I see the Devil in his corner
shaking his head not having to say anything
this time for a change.

Michael Estabrook has been publishing his poetry in the small press since the 1980s. He has published over 20 collections, a recent one being *The Poet's Curse, A Miscellany* (The Poetry Box, 2019). He lives in Acton, Massachusetts.

In Particular Light
Brian Builta

You walk drunk into the park one night
after hours with your brother who
is not your brother but who is now
your brother and there she is: the officer
who is kicking you out of the park who
is the officer who cut your son down
from his bunk that day. She recognizes you
as a bad shift, the opposite of velvet.
She asks about your family but avoids
the blast zone she'll not forget.
Your brother is crouching as if to puke
but keeps it together. Now you wish
you were a daymoon, anywhere but dark
as she ushers you out into the rest
of your life, which was not your life
but is now your life, this night
a kind of jewel that will sparkle
in particular light if you
look at it just right.

Brian Builta lives in Arlington, Texas, and works at Texas Wesleyan University in Fort Worth. He has recently published poems in *Jabberwock Review, Juke Joint Magazine, Rabid Oak, Triggerfish Critical Review* and *Unbroken Journal*, with poems forthcoming in *Thimble Literary Magazine, Main Street Rag* and *South Florida Poetry Journal.*

Breakfast with Bukowki
Bruce Robinson

i remember finding a volume
of Bukowski on the shelf, no idea
how it got there, big book, close to 300
pages, you could read it in the morning
without the light on, yes, easy reading,
easier than the paper, no, not
drinking wine, just coffee with breakfast
and bukowski without the light on.

Recent work by **Bruce Robinson,** not wanted in the kitchen, appears or is forthcoming in *Tar River Poetry, Spoon River, Pangyrus, Maintenant, Shot Glass,* and *Mantis.* He lives in Brooklyn,

Willed to Science
Gene Twaronite

As I wander through this saguaro forest
of centenarians and nurse tree juveniles,
my gaze turns to the departed citizens
in different stages of death who,
unless removed by some graverobber
to become a lamp or a souvenir,
never truly leave, bodies riddled
with bullet holes or oozing black rot,
shrouded in brittle gray skin

over white spongy innards,
crumbling away to reveal
solemn silvery ribbed columns,
some sprung apart as if
there's nothing left
to hold them together,
suddenly released from
the tension of living.

Would that my body were not
promised to some medical student
I will never meet (alas)
to probe and dissect the plaques
and tangles of my brain
or whatever gets me in the end,
and that I could rest here instead
among these departed friends,
my withered innards slowly
disintegrating to reveal
my silvery rib cage
waiting for the desert
to take me back.

And wouldn't I make
a fine lamp?

Gene Twaronite is the author of four collections of poetry as well as the rhyming picture book *How to Eat Breakfast*. His first poetry book *Trash Picker on Mars*, published by Kelsay Books, was the winner of the 2017 New Mexico-Arizona Book Award for Arizona poetry. His newest poetry collection *Shopping Cart Dreams* will be published by Kelsay Books in 2022. Gene's poems have been described as: "ranging from edgy to whimsical to inscrutable … playfully haunting and hauntingly playful." A former New Englander, Gene now lives in Tucson. Follow more of his poetry at genetwaronite.poet.com

Dyscalculia
Christian Ward

The walking stick stammers
across the bus seat's abacus frame
like an equation trying to solve itself
fifty years too late.

Christian Ward is a UK-based writer who can be recently found in *Red Ogre Review*, *Discretionary Love* and *Stone Poetry Journal*. Future poems will be appearing in *Dreich*, *Uppagus* and *BlueHouse Journal*.

Freefall
Robert Estes

It's simple,
once you think of it.
If I jump off
a tall building
with no restraint,
I'm continually
accelerated
downward
(weightless,
weightless),
and, as I fall,
the interval of time
between my seeing
into one floor's windows
and those of the
next one
lower down
decreases
the whole while;
the hint seems clear:
there has to be

another time
through which we fall,
from birth,
in what
we call time,
thus to experience
the events
of our lives
ever more closely packed.
Embedded
in Eternity,
they wait
for us to
plummet

past.

Robert Estes, who lives in Somerville, Massachusetts, got his PhD in Physics at UC Berkeley and had some interesting times doing physics, notably on a couple of US-Italian Space Shuttle missions. His poems have recently appeared in *The Moth, Gargoyle, The Main Street Rag, Third Wednesday, Evening Street Review, SLANT, Blue Unicorn,* and the anthology *Moving Images: Poetry Inspired by Cinema.*

Goalie

William Heath

I crouch on my toes
before the goal knowing
at what speed a kicked ball
can humiliate ten useless
sausages I use for fingers
and the dinosaurian pace
a message reaches the brain.
The enemy throw triumphant
hands in the air, hug each other
as if the war were over,
while I turn to retrieve
the white sphere that lies
behind me on the ground
at the back of the net
as docile as a skull.

Fascist Kitsch
William Heath

Each insurrection has its aesthetics.
Trump's cult, in a deep state of delusion,
storms the Capitol to stop the theft of
an election Biden won by seven million.
They come in outlandish costumes,
in combat camouflage tactical gear
as if on a special ops mission,
others cosplaying characters of choice:
Vikings, Goth invaders, Good Old Boys
primed for a plastered tailgate party.
Whatever the outfit, all are armed
with I-phones to live-stream selfie-shots
to co-conspirators across the country.

This is the politics of spectacle,
mad mayhem as performance theater,
acting out a video game where real
blood is shed. Smugly gleeful faces
show how they feel to trash a world
they do not understand. Fantasies
can be dangerous, kitsch can kill,
Trump has whipped his fascist thugs
into a red-hatted rage that ignores
the forces wrecking their lives.
In the name of "freedom" they
stab a dagger in our democracy,
bring lasting harm and shame.

William Heath lives in Maryland and has published two books of poems, *The Walking Man* and *Steel Valley Elegy*; two chapbooks, *Night Moves in Ohio* and *Leaving Seville*; three novels: *The Children Bob Moses Led* (winner of the Hackney Award), *Devil Dancer*, and *Blacksnake's Path*; a work of history, *William Wells and the Struggle for the Old Northwest* (winner of two Spur Awards); and a collection of interviews, *Conversations with Robert Stone*. www.williamheathbooks.com

Fully-Extended Lawn-Chair Back-Porch Star-Gazing Meditation
James Eric Watkins

I fully extend my self into this lawn chair,
gaze up in meditation from my back porch
and into this hazy white, blue night
deep space light —

Smoke curls, swirls,
ascends from my lips
like spirits from the earth,
gathers in clouds of contemplation.

The higher they rise,
the thinner and more wispy
the thoughts become, until dissipation:
changing from something to nothing to everything.

Tiny yellow horseweed blooms burst
and scatter their pollen on the porch rail.
Tall plants sway against a starry night backdrop.

The wind licks my bare skin
like a lover.
And my senses become alive.

I see three suns die.
On the dark surface
of the night, trails of light
write their final expressions
across the sky . . . tapering into everything.

James Eric Watkins has dramatically performed his poetry at the Madison-Jefferson County (Indiana) Public Library, the University of Southern Indiana, and at Indiana University Southeast, as well as at the Village Lights Bookstore in Madison, Indiana and other venues. James' creative work has appeared in *Acorn, The Scioto Voice Newspaper, The Main Street Rag, Pegasus, Tipton Poetry Journal, Visions, Moments of the Soul* and many others. He is a 2021 Touchstone Award Nominee and a 2021 Pushcart Prize Nominee. James is the editor and publisher of *Promise of Light Publications/Flowers & Vortexes Creative Magazine*.

One True Faith
Dan Carpenter

At the stroke of midnight
Monsignor rises to a silent summons
raises shaking hands
that shook yours after
they broke the Bread
and breaches the bedroom portal
to the stars and slice of moon
to find himself in another hemisphere
at last and for the first time at prayer
five times daily with his brother men
as his tea and his bed are prepared
in a house that never will fall silent
or go cold or lose fragrance
under care of a woman
who calls him by given name
never Father in company
sometimes Child in private
who knows God's permission
in this place and no other on Earth
to shed their robes

Dan Carpenter has published poetry and fiction in *Illuminations, Pearl, Poetry East, Southern Indiana Review, Maize, Flying Island, Pith, The Laurel Review, Sycamore Review, Prism International, Fiction, Hopewell Review* and other journals. A collection of columns written for *The Indianapolis Star*, where he earns his living, was published by Indiana University Press in 1993 with the title *Hard Pieces: Dan Carpenter's Indiana*. Dan also contributed to the IU Press books *Falling Toward Grace* (1998) and *Urban Tapestry* (2002) and wrote the text for the photo book *Indiana 24/7 (DK Publishing, 2004)*.
photo book *Indiana 24/7 (DK Publishing, 2004)*.

The Monks of the Drepung Losing Monastery Visit the WSU Art Gallery

Nancy Kay Peterson

Tibetan monks in maroon and saffron and worn Minnetonka moccasins don headdresses and play their long horns and cymbals and bells and chant in tones that vibrate through space and time. One draws the outline for the sand Mandala with white chalk and a K-Mart compass. Others set out Tupperware for colored sands poured from Zip-Lock Baggies. Another unrolls a cotton cloth holding dented funnels that will channel world healing and universal peace to Winona, Minnesota. As if men hold heaven in their hands.

Nancy Kay Peterson's poetry has appeared in print and online in numerous publications, most recently in *Dash Literary Journal, HerWords, Last Stanza Poetry Journal, One Sentence Poems, Spank the Carp, Steam Ticket, Tipton Poetry Journal and Three Line Poetry*. From 2004-2009, she co-edited and co-published *Main Channel Voices: A Dam Fine Literary Magazine* (Winona, Minnesota). Finishing Line Press published her two poetry chapbooks, *Belated Remembrance* (2010) and *Selling the Family* (2021). For more information, see www.nancykaypeterson.com.

Tomato Pincushions
Virginia Watts

My mother had one, aunts, great aunts.
I inherited seven. They cling together inside
a kitchen drawer. My grandmother's is pink,
faded by sewing room window sun. Once
she nearly swallowed a pin pursed between
her lips when dynamite blasted another
hole inside the coal mine. Her fingers
flew from the Singer to save her. I never
plucked any flat, silver pinheads from
my grandmother's pincushion, the steel
spines remain just where she placed them.

I run the whole holiday show now instead
of her, invitations, mood music, dusted
punch bowl, well-seasoned turkey,
and this year, tomato pincushions
strung by tattered leaves in lighted
tree. My grandmother's shines
brightest, a dime dropped in a gritty
alley of a quiet town with a quiet mine.
In a few days, another crystal ball
will fall to her knees in Times Square.

Virginia Watts lives in Pennsylvania and is the author of poetry and stories found in *Illuminations, The Florida Review, CRAFT, Two Hawks Quarterly, Hawaii Pacific Review, Sky Island Journal, Permafrost Magazine, Wisconsin Review, Pithead Chapel, Dark Lane Anthology Series* among others. Winner of the 2019 *Florida Review* Meek Award in nonfiction, two of her poetry chapbooks are available from Moonstone Press and a short story collection is upcoming from The Devil's Party Press. She has been nominated three times for a Pushcart Prize and three times for Best of the Net.

Review: Time and Tide: An Atlas for the Grieving *by Denise Thompson-Slaughter*

Reviewed by Barry Harris

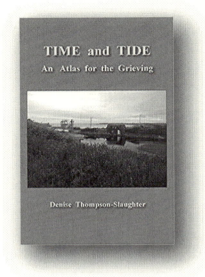

Title: *Time and Tide: An Atlas for the Grieving*

Author: Denise Thompson-Slaughter

Year: 2021

Publisher: Plain View Press

Denise Thompson-Slaughter's newest chapbook, *Time and Tide: An Atlas for the Grieving,* opens with "Against the Tide," a poem about the loss of the author's son. As one expects, the poem is poignant and we are caught up with the poet in her understandable and unimaginable grief.

> At the spot where the land took you,
> I hang on to the pier,
> arms wrapped tight around a wooden pylon
> connecting earth to the river of time.

The opening sets the scene not only for this poem but for the entire chapbook. We can only imagine the strength it takes to hang desperately to the physical site of the poet's tragic loss of her son. The mother and poet vows that she "will not leave the spot where you disappeared," but soon she describes how time stops within the grieving process and despite dream visitations, slowly "the raucous river is full of new water, new life, new eddies and sites of interest, even to me."

The poem concludes with:

> My grip loosens and the waves pull me from my post,
> wash me further downstream
> with my hands full of splinters,
> bobbing like a cork,
> anchorless.

The next few poems deal with a mother's loss with personal, painful questions like "Why are you not here to talk about the race for President?" or

> Why are you not here to discuss the news or metaphysics,
> to critique our parenting,
> carry our boxes up and down the stairs?
> ... Why are you not here to watch the Superbowl with your poor brokenhearted father?

In "Dream from Raindrop Lake," Thompson-Slaughter reminds herself that life

> is but a dream,
> one entering its final REM stage, I hope,
> because I am oh so tired of
> row row rowing my boat.

But soon the sudden but lasting grief of a mother for a lost child is enveloped by the grief of a world just as suddenly gripped by the COVID pandemic. In "Covid 19-20, New York CIty," the author who lives in New York State, reports on the efforts in the city and state to cope with the rapid early push of the pandemic:

> New York has already lost the first five hundred voters.
> There will be tens of thousands more.

A mother's loss has morphed into the continuing world's losses. Denise Thompson-Slaughter extends her insights from personal grief into a short atlas for all the grieving. In "The Quick & the Dead," she begins to advise us with metaphysical lessons:

When your dead outnumber your quick
and you can't imagine what's left to do,
you perhaps will know this fancy to be true:
Time is a slippery eel of delusion....
When finally your ship arrives, heralded
by the parting of angels, eels or other creatures
of the high and low dimensions,
you will embark with relief...
as they strain to see you beyond the growing mist.
They are trapped in time and cannot perceive you.

You can see everything.

While ultimately, the poems included in *Time and Tide* are essentially hopeful, there is no magic formula as Denise points out in her poem, "The Club No One Wants to Belong To:"

Whether robbed by disease, suicide, accident, or violence,
all of us dwell in rooms of earthly hell
with only paper-thin walls between us,
our nerve endings raw and invisibly twitching...
Don't you get sick of everyone saying
"I don't know how you do it?"
There is no how.
There is only to die or to keep breathing...
But the only superpower you've got
is putting one foot in front of the other.
So,
we do it again today.

Denise Thompson-Slaughter is an author living in western New York State. Her previous published works include two books of poetry, *Elemental,* (Plain View Press, 2010), and *Sixty-ish: Full Circle,* (Spirited Muse Press, 2017); a mystery novella *Mystery Gifts,* (Spirited Muse Press, 2018) and non-fction *Cleaning the Coincidence Closet: Exploring the Inexplicable* (lulu.com, 2021).

Barry Harris is editor of the *Tipton Poetry Journal* and four anthologies by Brick Street Poetry. He has published one poetry collection, *Something At The Center*.

Married and father of two grown sons, Barry lives in Brownsburg, Indiana and is retired from Eli Lilly and Company.

His poetry has appeared in *Kentucky Review, Valparaiso Poetry Review, Grey Sparrow, Silk Road Review, Saint Ann's Review, North Dakota Quarterly, Boston Literary Magazine, Night Train, Silver Birch Press, Flying Island, Awaken Consciousness, Writers' Bloc, Red-Headed Stepchild* and *Laureate: The Literary Journal of Arts for Lawrence*.

He graduated a long time ago with a major in English from Ball State University.

Review of *Open Secrets: The Ultimate Guide to Marketing Your Book* by Tupelo Press
Reviewed by Joyce Brinkman

Title: *Open Secrets: The Ultimate Guide to Marketing Your Book*

Author: Tupelo Press

Year: 2021

Publisher: Tupelo Press

As a writer while browsing through reviews of new books you might ask yourself why would I want to buy a book titled *Open Secrets The Ultimate Guild to Marketing Your Book*. The title has told you there are no mysteries in this book, and the title is right. This book does not present new ideas but what it does do is get you thinking about marketing which is something that every writer needs to do. It brings the most effective marketing ideas together in one place and provides guidance for your development of a marketing plan.

I do a workshop called Putting on the Writer's Caps. Please notice it is Caps with an "s" not cap. Too often writers think their only job is to write. That workshop and this book tell you otherwise. You already believe you're a good writer. After all, a worthy publisher wants to publish your book, so you have the first ingredient in marketing success believing in the product. People who don't believe in what they're marketing can't sustain the effort needed to make it a success.

It's easy to think "I'm not good at marketing", but as this book point out that no one is better because no one knows your book better than you. You are the expert on your book. You love it and when you plan to use the marketing techniques that we all know work, you will do the best job of selling your book. Realizing that and preparing your plan is key to your success. *Open Secrets The Ultimate Guild to Marketing Your Book* skillfully drives that point home while giving you proven insights on how to develop your plan.

This book starts you on your marketing quest by having you focus first on just who your market is. Personally, I think this is valuable before you even start your book. Holding a market in mind can actually help shape a book. A writer should understand who she is writing for. If she's really writing for herself it may have value but is may also have a very small market.

When you've identified your market, developed your plan and are convinced that you know your product best you are ready for success. The enthusiastic use of the well organized methods of reaching that market in this book will produce results. The size of your market will depend on your forethought in targeting and your commitment to your plan. How to do that is a very "open secret" skillfully assembled and waiting within this helpful book's pages.

Joyce Brinkman, Indiana Poet Laureate 2002-2008, believes in poetry as public art. She creates public poetry projects involving her poetry and the poetry of others. Collaborations with visual artists using her poetry for permanent installations include her words in a twenty-five foot stained glass window by British glass artist Martin Donlin at the Indianapolis International Airport, in lighted glass by Arlon Bayliss at the Indianapolis-Marion County Central Library and on a wall with local El Salvadoran artists in the town square of Quezaltepeque, El Salvador.

Her printed works include two chapbooks, *Tiempo Español*, and *Nine Poems In Form Nine*, and two collaborative books, *Rivers, Rails and Runways*, and *Airmail from the Airpoets* from San Francisco Bay Press, with fellow "airpoets" Ruthelen Burns, Joe Heithaus, and Norbert Krapf.

Her latest books include the multinational, multilingual book *Seasons of Sharing A Kasen Renku Collaboration, from Leapfrog Press, Urban Voices: 51 Poems from 51 American Poets* from San Francisco Bay Press, which she co-edited with Carolyn Kreiter-Foronda and *Elizabeth Barrett Browning Illuminated by the Message* from ACTA Publications.

Joyce organized the collaborative poems for the Indiana Bicentennial Legacy Book *Mapping the Muse* from Brick Street Poetry. She recently completed a public art project in Martinsville, Indiana, featuring poetry she wrote inspired by the life and words of UCLA basketball coach and Hoosier native John Wooden. Joyce is the producer of the poetry podcast "Off the Bricks", which can be heard on Spotify and other podcast platforms or through the Brick Street Poetry website http://brickstreetpoetry.org. Joyce is a graduate of Hanover College and resides in Zionsville, Indiana, with a cantankerous cat.

Editor

Barry Harris is editor of the *Tipton Poetry Journal* and four anthologies by Brick Street Poetry: *Mapping the Muse: A Bicentennial Look at Indiana Poetry; Words and Other Wild Things* and *Cowboys & Cocktails: Poems from the True Grit Saloon,* and *Reflections on Little Eagle Creek.* He has published one poetry collection, *Something At The Center.*

Married and father of two grown sons, Barry lives in Brownsburg, Indiana and is retired from Eli Lilly and Company.

His poetry has appeared in *Kentucky Review, Valparaiso Poetry Review, Grey Sparrow, Silk Road Review, Saint Ann's Review, North Dakota Quarterly, Boston Literary Magazine, Night Train, Silver Birch Press, Flying Island, Awaken Consciousness, Writers' Bloc, Red-Headed Stepchild* and *Laureate: The Literary Journal of Arts for Lawrence.* One of his poems was on display at the National Museum of Sport and another is painted on a barn in Boone County, Indiana as part of Brick Street Poetry's Word Hunger public art project. His poems are also included in these anthologies: *From the Edge of the Prairie; Motif 3: All the Livelong Day;* and *Twin Muses: Art and Poetry.*

He graduated a long time ago with a major in English from Ball State University.

Tipton Poetry Journal

Contributor Biographies

Gil Arzola is the second son of a migrant worker living in Valparaiso, Indiana with his wife Linda. He was named Poet Of The Year by Passager Press in 2019. His first book of poetry *Prayers of Little Consequence* was published in 2020. Rattle published a chapbook *The Death of Migrant Worker* in September of 2021 after selecting it from 2000 submissions for their annual prize. A story *Losers Walk,* originally published by Chaluer, was nominated for a Pushcart Award in 2018. His work has appeared in *Whetstone, Palabra, Crosswinds, Tipton Poetry Journal, Passager, Slab* and *The Elysian Review* among others.

Victoria Woolf Bailey lives in Kentucky and is recently retired. Her first full-length collection, *Cannibalism and the Copenhagen Interpretation: a Love Story* will be released in March 2022 by Finishing Line Press.

Raised on a rice and catfish farm in eastern Arkansas, **CL Bledso**e is the author of more than twenty books, including the poetry collections *Riceland, Trashcans in Love, Grief Bacon,* and his newest, *Driving Around, Looking in Other People's Windows,* as well as his latest novels *Goodbye, Mr. Lonely* and the forthcoming *The Saviors.* Bledsoe co-writes the humor blog *How to Even,* with Michael Gushue located here: https://medium.com/@howtoeven. His own blog, *Not Another TV Dad,* is located here: https://medium.com/@clbledsoe. He's been published in hundreds of journals, newspapers, and websites that you've probably never heard of. Bledsoe lives in northern Virginia with his daughter.

Leah Browning lives in California and is the author of three short nonfiction books and six chapbooks of poetry and fiction. Her work has recently appeared in *Four Way Review, The Broadkill Review, Oyster River Pages, The Forge Literary Magazine, The Threepenny Review, Valparaiso Fiction Review, Watershed Review, Random Sample Review, Belletrist Magazine, Poetry South, The Stillwater Review, Superstition Review, Santa Ana River Review, Newfound, The Homestead Review, Bellows American Review, Coldnoon, Clementine Unbound, The Literary Review*, and elsewhere. www.leahbrowninglit.com

Cindy Buchanan grew up in Alaska and has lived in Seattle since graduating from Gonzaga. Work has been published in *Evening Street Review, The MacGuffin, Rabid Oak, Hole in the Head Review,* and *Chestnut Review,* and is upcoming in *Main Street Rag.* An avid runner and hiker with a deep interest in Buddhist philosophy and Zen meditation practice, she has completed the Camino de Santiago in Spain, the Coast to Coast Walk in England, and the Milford Walking Track in New Zealand.

Brian Builta lives in Arlington, Texas, and works at Texas Wesleyan University in Fort Worth. He has recently published poems in *Jabberwock Review, Juke Joint Magazine, Rabid Oak, Triggerfish Critical Review* and *Unbroken Journal,* with poems forthcoming in *Thimble Literary Magazine, Main Street Rag* and *South Florida Poetry Journal.*

Dan Carpenter has published poetry and fiction in *Illuminations, Pearl, Poetry East, Southern Indiana Review, Maize, Flying Island, Pith, The Laurel Review, Sycamore Review, Prism International, Fiction, Hopewell Review* and other journals. A collection of columns written for *The Indianapolis Star*, where he earns his living, was published by Indiana University Press in 1993 with the title *Hard Pieces: Dan Carpenter's Indiana*. Dan also contributed to the IU Press books *Falling Toward Grace* (1998) and *Urban Tapestry* (2002) and wrote the text for the photo book *Indiana 24/7 (DK Publishing, 2004)*. photo book *Indiana 24/7 (DK Publishing, 2004)*.

Wendy Cleveland is a retired NYS high school English teacher who now teaches an ekphrastic poetry class for the Auburn University lifelong learning program, and a member of the Alabama Writers' Forum. Her work has appeared in *Persimmon Tree, Red Rock Review,* and *Glass Mountain,* among other journals. In 2016 Solomon & George published her poetry collection, *Blue Ford.*

Gayle Compton, a hillbilly from Eastern Kentucky, lives up the river from where Randall McCoy is buried and attended college on the hill where "Cotton Top" Mounts was hanged. With deep affection, he tells the story of Appalachia's common people, allowing them to speak, without apology, in their own colorful language. His prize-winning stories, poems, and essays have appeared most recently in *Sow's Ear, Now and Then, New Southerner, Blue Collar Review, Kentucky Review,* and *Main Street Rag* anthologies.

After 34 years with Eli Lilly and Company, **Brendan Crowley** set up his own consulting and executive coaching business, Brendan Crowley Advisors LLC. He helps executives grow in their roles and careers. Brendan is originally from Ireland and lives with his wife Rosaleen in Zionsville, Indiana. He has a passion for photography and loves taking photographs of his home country, Ireland, and here in Indiana.

Tammy Daniel was selected as one of New Voices of 2015 by The Writers Place in Kansas City, Missouri. She was a finalist in the Davis Grove Haiku and Nature Poetry Contest, and her work has appeared in *I-70 Review, Touch: The Journal of Healing, The Ekphrastic Review, Anthology on Aging: The Shining Years, Dying Dahlia Review, Wild Goose Poetry Review, Red River Review, Rusty Truck, Ink Sweat and Tears*, and the Johnson County Library.

EG Ted Davis is a semi-retiree who resides in Boise, Idaho and has written poetry since back in the 80's with work appearing in various online literary journals and websites in the US and the UK.

Michael Estabrook has been publishing his poetry in the small press since the 1980s. He has published over 20 collections, a recent one being *The Poet's Curse, A Miscellany* (The Poetry Box, 2019). He lives in Acton, Massachusetts.

Robert Estes, who lives in Somerville, Massachusetts, got his PhD in Physics at UC Berkeley and had some interesting times doing physics, notably on a couple of US-Italian Space Shuttle missions. His poems have recently appeared in *The Moth, Gargoyle, The Main Street Rag, Third Wednesday, Evening Street Review, SLANT, Blue Unicorn*, and the anthology *Moving Images: Poetry Inspired by Cinema.*

Caroline Fernandez is an Indo-Canadian journalist and performer based in Dubai. Her reporting has ranged from media analysis to arts, business, and culture, and she has also contributed to and led several social justice projects around sexuality and inequality. She has been published in various news publications including *TimeOut Dubai, toronto.com* and *Communicate*. She's performed on stages across Toronto, Montreal, Bangalore and Dubai. She is also the founder of the multimedia news platform *Kerosene Digital*. Currently she is an MFA candidate at Vermont College and is working on a collection of essays and poetry.

Sergey Gerasimov is a Ukraine-based writer. His stories and poems have appeared in *Adbusters, Clarkesworld Magazine, Strange Horizons, J Journal, Triggerfish Critical Review*, among others. His last book is *Oasis* published by Gypsy Shadow.

James Green has worked as a naval officer, deputy sheriff, high school English teacher, professor of education, and administrator in both public schools and universities. Recipient of two Fulbright grants, he has served as a visiting scholar at the University of Limerick in Ireland and the National Chung Cheng University in Taiwan. In addition to academic publications, including three books, Green is the author of three chapbooks of poetry and a fourth, *Long Journey Home*, is forthcoming after winning the Charles Dickson Chapbook Contest sponsored by the Georgia Poetry Society., Individual poems have appeared in literary magazines in England, Ireland, and the United States. He resides in Muncie, Indiana.

Michael Gushue is co-founder of the nanopress *Poetry Mutual*. His books are *Pachinko Mouth* (Plan B Press), *Conrad* (Silver Spoon Press), *Gathering Down Women* (Pudding House Press), and—in collaboration with CL Bledsoe—*I Never Promised You A Sea Monkey* (Pretzelcoatl Press). He lives in the Brookland neighborhood of Washington, D.C.

Jean Harper's writing has appeared in *The Florida Review, North American Review, Iowa Review*, and elsewhere. She is has received fellowships from the National Endowment for the Arts, the Indiana Arts Commission, and been in residence at Yaddo, MacDowell, and the Virginia Center for the Creative Arts. She lives in northeast Indiana.

William Heath lives in Maryland and has published two books of poems, *The Walking Man* and *Steel Valley Elegy*; two chapbooks, *Night Moves in Ohio* and *Leaving Seville*; three novels: *The Children Bob Moses Led* (winner of the Hackney Award), *Devil Dancer*, and *Blacksnake's Path*; a work of history, *William Wells and the Struggle for the Old Northwest* (winner of two Spur Awards); and a collection of interviews, *Conversations with Robert Stone*. www.williamheathbooks.com

Claire Keyes is the author of two collections of poetry: *The Question of Rapture* (Mayapple Press) and *What Diamonds Can Do* (WordTech). Her chapbook, *Rising and Falling*, won the Foothills Poetry Competition. Professor Emerita at Salem State University, she lives in Marblehead, Massachusetts and her poems have been published recently in *Mom Egg Review, Turtle Island, One Art,* and *Persimmon Tree*.

A former Indiana Poet Laureate, **Norbert Krapf** has published fourteen poetry collections, the most recent *Indiana Hill Country Poems* and *Southwest by Midwest. My Homecomings: A Writer's Memoir*, covering the fifty years of his writing and publishing life, will appear next year. Krapf has also produced a poetry and jazz CD with pianist-composer Monika Herzig, *Imagine* and also performs poetry and blues with Gordon Bonham. See also www.krapfpoetry.net.

Having retired from teaching English and Communications, first in the US and for many years in Jamaica, **Mary Hills Kuck** now lives with her family in Massachusetts. She has received a Pushcart Prize Nomination and her poems have appeared in *Connecticut River Review, Hamden Chronicle, SIMUL: Lutheran Voices in Poetry, Caduceus, The Jamaica Observer Bookends, Fire Stick: A Collection of New & Established Caribbean Poets, the Aurorean, Tipton Poetry Journal, Burningwood Literary Journal, Slant* and *Main Street Rag*, and others.

Bruce Levine, a 2019 Pushcart Prize Poetry Nominee, has spent his life as a writer of fiction and poetry and as a music and theatre professional. Over 300 of his works are published in over 25 on-line journals including *Ariel Chart, Friday Flash Fiction, Literary Yard;* over 30 print books including *Poetry Quarterly, Haiku Journal, Dual Coast Magazine*, and his shows have been produced in New York and around the country. Six eBooks are available from Amazon.com. His work is dedicated to the loving memory of his late wife, Lydia Franklin. He lives in Maine with his dog, Daisy. Visit him at www.brucelevine.com.

George Looney is the founder of the BFA in Creative Writing Program at Penn State Erie, editor-in-chief of the international literary journal *Lake Effect*, translation editor of *Mid-American Review*, and co-founder of the original Chautauqua Writers' Festival. He has published several books, most recently *The Itinerate Circus: New and Selected Poems 1995-2020 (Red Mountain Press, 2020), The Worst May Be Over (Elixer Press, 2020), and Ode to the Earth in Translation (Red Mountain Press, 2021).*

Marianne Lyon has been a music teacher for 43 years. After teaching in Hong Kong she returned to the Napa Valley and has been published in various literary magazines and reviews. Nominated for the Pushcart Award 2016. She has spent time teaching in Nicaragua. She is a member of the California Writers Club, Solstice Writers in St. Helena California and an Adjunct Professor at Touro University Vallejo California. She was awarded the Napa Country Poet Laureate 2021 title.

Karla Linn Merrifield Karla Linn Merrifield has had 900+ poems appear in dozens of journals and anthologies. She has 14 books to her credit. Following her 2018 *Psyche's Scroll* (Poetry Box Select) is the 2019 full-length book *Athabaskan Fractal: Poems of the Far North* from Cirque Press. She is currently at work on a poetry collection, *My Body the Guitar*, inspired by famous guitarists and their guitars; the book is slated to be published in December 2021 by Before Your Quiet Eyes Publications Holograph Series (Rochester, NY).

Cecil Morris lives in California and is retired after 37 years of teaching high school English. He now tries writing himself what he spent so many years teaching others to understand and enjoy. He likes ice Cream too much and cruciferous vegetables too little. He has had a handful of poems published in *2River View, Cobalt Review, English Journal, The Ekphrastic Review, The Midwest Quarterly, Poem*, and other literary magazines.

Jennifer Novotney's work appears in *Buddhist Poetry Review, The Beatnik Cowboy,* and *The Vignette Review*, where she was nominated for a Pushcart Prize. She won the 2014 Moonbeam Children's Book Award for her novel, *Winter in the Soul*. She lives in Pennsylvania where she teaches English at a small independent school.

Fasasi Abdulrosheed Oladipupo is a Nigerian poet and a Veterinary Medical Student at University of Ibadan, whose first love is art making. His poems were nominated for the 2021 BOTN and for the 2021 Pushcart Prize. He is an avid reader, who sees poetry in everything, with great interest in storytelling. His works have appeared, or are forthcoming in: *Southern Humanities Review, Oxford Review of Books, Oakland Arts Review, Scrawl Place, Short Vine Journal, Cathexis Northwest Press, South Florida Poetry Journal, Olongo Africa, Roanoke Review, Watershed Review, Panoplyzine, Kissing Dynamite, The Night Heron Barks Review, The Citron Review, Stand Magazine, Louisiana Literature, Obsidian: Literature and Art in the African Diaspora, Welter Journal, Praxis Magazine* and elsewhere.

Born in the Caribbean and raised in the U.S., **Tia Paul-Louis** began writing songs at age 11 then experimented with poetry during high school. She earned a BA in English/Creative Writing from the University of South Florida along with a M.F.A in Creative Writing from National University in California. Her works have appeared in literary magazines such as *The Voices Project, Ethos Literary Journal,* and *Rabbit Catastrophe Review*. Some of her favorite authors and poets include Langston Hughes, Emily Dickinson, Maya Angelou and Edgar Allan Poe. Apart from writing, Paul-Louis enjoys music, photography, acting and cooking, though she mostly finds herself and others through poetry.

Nancy Kay Peterson's poetry has appeared in print and online in numerous publications, most recently in *Dash Literary Journal, HerWords, Last Stanza Poetry Journal, One Sentence Poems, Spank the Carp, Steam Ticket, Tipton Poetry Journal and Three Line Poetry*. From 2004-2009, she co-edited and co-published *Main Channel Voices: A Dam Fine Literary Magazine* (Winona, Minnesota). Finishing Line Press published her two poetry chapbooks, *Belated Remembrance* (2010) and *Selling the Family* (2021). For more information, see www.nancykaypeterson.com.

Kenneth Pobo is the author of 21 chapbooks and 9 full-length collections. Recent books include *Bend of Quiet* (Blue Light Press), *Loplop in a Red City* (Circling Rivers), *Dindi Expecting Snow* (Duck Lake Books), *Wingbuds* (cyberwit.net), and *Uneven Steven* (Assure Press). *Opening* from Rectos Y Versos Editions is forthcoming. Human rights issues, especially as they relate to the LGBTQIA+ community, are also a constant presence in his work. In addition to poetry, he also writes fiction and essays. For the past thirty-plus years he taught at Widener University in Pennsylvania and retired in 2020.

Patrick T. Reardon, a three-time Pushcart Prize nominee living in Chicago, is the author of nine books, including the poetry collection *Requiem for David* and *Faith Stripped to Its Essence*. His poetry has appeared in *America, Rhino, Main Street Rag, The Write Launch, Meat for Tea, Under a Warm Green Linden* and many others. He has two poetry collections in 2021: *Puddin: The Autobiography of a Baby, a Memoir in Prose-poems* (Third World Press) and *Darkness on the Face of the Deep* (Kelsay Books).

Timothy Robbins has been teaching English as a Second Language for 30 years. His poems have appeared in many literary journals and has published five volumes of poetry: *Three New Poets* (Hanging Loose Press), *Denny's Arbor Vitae* (Adelaide Books), *Carrying Bodies* (Main Street Rag Press) *Mother Wheel* (Cholla Needles Press) and *This Night I Sup in Your House* (Cyberwit.net). He lives in Wisconsin with his husband of 24 years.

Recent work by **Bruce Robinson,** not wanted in the kitchen, appears or is forthcoming in *Tar River Poetry, Spoon River, Pangyrus, Maintenant, Shot Glass,* and *Mantis*. He lives in Brooklyn, New York.

Mary Sexson is the author of *103 in the Light, Selected Poems 1996-200* (Restoration Press, 2004) and coauthor of *Company of Women, New and Selected Poems*, (Chatter House Press, 2013). A 3 time Pushcart Prize nominee, her poetry appears or is forthcoming in *Flying Island, New Verse News, The World We Live(d) In, Hoosier Lit, Last Stanza Poetry Journal, High Veld Poetry Review,* and *Anti-Heroin Chic*. Her poetry is part of the INverse Poetry Archive, a collection of poetry by Indiana poets, housed at the Indiana State Library.

Christopher Stolle's writing has appeared most recently in *Tipton Poetry Journal, Flying Island, Last Stanza Poetry Journal, The New Southern Fugitives, The Alembic, Gravel, The Light Ekphrastic, Sheepshead Review,* and *Plath Poetry Project*. He's an editor for DK Publishing and he lives in Richmond, Indiana.

Michael E. Strosahl is a midwestern river-born poet, originally from Moline, Illinois, now living in Jefferson City, Missouri. Besides several appearances in the *Tipton Poetry Journal*, Maik's work has appeared in *Flying Island, Bards Against Hunger* projects, on buses, in museums and online at *indianavoicejournal, poetrysuperhighway* and *projectagentorange*. Maik also has a weekly poetry column at the online blog *Moristotle & Company*.

Allison Thorpe lives in Lexington, Kentucky. Her collection, *Reckless Pilgrims*, was published in 2021 by Broadstone Books.

Gene Twaronite is a Tucson poet and the author of ten books. His first poetry collection *Trash Picker on Mars* (Kelsay Books) was the winner of the 2017 New Mexico-Arizona Book Award for Arizona poetry. Recent poetry collections include *The Museum of Unwearable Shoes* and *What the Gargoyle Sees* (Kelsay Books).
Follow more of his writing @thetwaronitezone.com.

Christian Ward is a UK-based writer who can be recently found in *Red Ogre Review, Discretionary Love* and *Stone Poetry Journal*. Future poems will be appearing in *Dreich, Uppagus* and *BlueHouse Journal*.

James Eric Watkins has dramatically performed his poetry at the Madison-Jefferson County (Indiana) Public Library, the University of Southern Indiana, and at Indiana University Southeast, as well as at the Village Lights Bookstore in Madison, Indiana and other venues. James' creative work has appeared in *Acorn, The Scioto Voice Newspaper, The Main Street Rag, Pegasus, Tipton Poetry Journal, Visions, Moments of the Soul* and many others. He is a 2021 Touchstone Award Nominee and a 2021 Pushcart Prize Nominee. James is the editor and publisher of *Promise of Light Publications/Flowers & Vortexes Creative Magazine*.

Virginia Watts lives in Pennsylvania and is the author of poetry and stories found in *Illuminations, The Florida Review, CRAFT, Two Hawks Quarterly, Hawaii Pacific Review, Sky Island Journal, Permafrost Magazine, Wisconsin Review, Pithead Chapel, Dark Lane Anthology Series* among others. Winner of the 2019 *Florida Review* Meek Award in nonfiction, two of her poetry chapbooks are available from Moonstone Press and a short story collection is upcoming from The Devil's Party Press. She has been nominated three times for a Pushcart Prize and three times for Best of the Net.

Marie Gray Wise lives in New Jersey. She has been published previously in *Tipton Poetry Journal* and in *I-70 Review, English Journal, U.S. 1 Worksheets, The Café Review, Naugatuck River Review, The Paterson Literary Review* and *Grey Sparrow Journal*.

Made in the USA
Middletown, DE
19 January 2022